The Unheard Scorpion

Pooja Jain

Presentation by *BookLeaf Publishing*

Web: www.bookleafpub.com

E-mail: info@bookleafpub.com

ISBN: 9789357747547

First edition 2023

DEDICATION

In memory of my loving dog, Goldy who taught
me unconditional love and patience.

ACKNOWLEDGEMENT

If you're here
I thank-you
for you make this Scorpion feel heard.

Inception

I wish I could remember
the inception
not of the Universe
but the one where I cried as the world rejoiced
dwindling and swinging from one arm to another
my eyes shut tight as I feared
would they hold me still? More so, catch me if I
fall?
so used to my mother's womb, where I was held
in warmth
nothing ever since has felt more safe, more
secure.

Infancy

The stage of sanity
is at infancy
unperturbed by world's noise
imaginative mind at its best flight
however, hustle is still expected
sleep, eat, cry and poo
crawl and drop a tumbler or two
yet all mistakes glorious
unconditionally accepted and celebrated
by all Gods and demons alike!

IF AND ONLY!

It all started with the act of motivating
luring her into dreams of a beautiful life
If and Only she was a pretty bride!

Her wings knew no bounds;
seizing every opportunity around,
they warned– her freedom would be justified
If and Only she was a married wife!

Shining trophies piling up to her glory
they warned– she would have a successful
career, no doubt
If and Only she made her rotis round!

The "If's and Only" lynched her mind
leaving her entirely:
constructed and destructed,
groomed and scarred,
polished and tarnished,
all at once, at the same time.

Bright Shadows

Dark grey
hazel dim light
nothing seemed possibly alright
mind, a narrow avenue
heart, not bright
it was time to explore my sight

A step out of the box would widen my vision,
I learned this when I was in prison,
and so started the journey of my soul
and so I hit that beautiful road!

A torch, map and a winsome guide,
I reached a destination– no rules to abide,
while gazing at the moonlit stars in the dark blue
skies,
I realised how really tiny were my eyes

No more bruises on the edge of a knife,
My heart pumped back to life,
Nature relieved me out of fright
And redeemed me with a blissful sight

Now I know
every blackness hides layers of charm

we need to break those chains
run out in the barn
feel the very fragrance of it
attaboy!
freedom is a blessing in disguise
a pure joy!

He and the Other

He divides by caste
The other unites by food

He is seen while rallying
The other is seldom seen with glory

He stays inebriated
The other is enervated

He keeps winning
The other keeps running

He owns property and lands
The other is just a farmhand

He kills others yet gets all the fame and name
The other feeds the world and rests himself on a
bed of nails

The Tree Speaks!

Wounded
I stand here lonely
the rest- chopped off, dragged and thrown into a
huge lorry

I once heard you talk about staying rooted and
grounded
and yet,
uprooted and unearthed
you make profit off our axed bodies

I wouldn't boast
but I provide for you
nourishment and greens
or as you say on your Gram
a sense of being

I hope you return the favour
not for me
but your future generations to behold
cause everything that exists doesn't exist to be
sacrificed
for you
and for you alone

She said Goodbye!

On hopes she hopped on the roof of the plot
willful and reckless
to herself immense joy she brought
putting her feet together
she danced under the sun so hot
focused intensely on the blue eagle, she climbed
the ladder for one best shot

On little hopes she walked on the roof of the plot
willful and careful
to herself small joys she brought
putting her feet together
she walked under the sun so hot
focussed lightly on the eagle
she stood there and waited on a rock

With dead hopes, she dragged herself till the
roof of the plot
unwilling and hesitated
to herself some cuts and bleeds she brought
putting her feet together
she tried to stand still under the sun so hot
focussed on an identity lost
she jumped from the spot

Infinite

When you look up high
and you see them twinkling in the sky
for a minute, you would feel tiny
no matter how hard the feeling hits resistance
sometimes, it might just question your existence

And then suddenly, you would feel Infinite!

That's when you shall know
that you need to grow
apart and away from all that makes a furrow

Break
let the walls of fear fall,
that's when you shall know
it's okay to face dilemmas
everything's a little more icing on the cake
life's a rainbow
sunshine with a little rain

Self-Love

This deprivation of external validation
that you feel time and again
this suffering that drains you day and night, right
from head to toes
I hope it pushes you to love yourself harder

Self-love is a journey
the most chaotic one, by far

It starts with entering the woods
deep, dense and dark
there's still a sense of security
because you aren't yet that far

The breeze starts to give you the chills
you didn't know it would be so cold
without a sweater vest, you feel so exposed
this vulnerability makes you even more prone
to the unknown and the unseen ever before

When you cannot decide where to go next
the quicksand of insecurities gets a grip on your
legs
you squeak in fear while trying to catch a breath
a native reaches out to hold your head

Traumatized by the horror
you lie still on the ground
there's no self-love
when you see your life
re-run in front of your eyes

You can't keep going, you're absolutely numb
but, the native tells you
you haven't come this far to stop right here

You stand back up
but you're still a little weak in the knees,
you drag your feet
a few last steps, that's what you tell yourself
though, it's blurry from a distance
you spot clear, a long grey tunnel

Now you've read about
there being light
at the end of a tunnel
hurriedly, you rush into it and walk a few miles
you see no exit, it's all twisted
you think it's a trap
the entry of the tunnel closes behind your back

You feel doomed, your back is against the wall
everything weighs you down, those tears finally
roll down

you sit there for hours, staring into the
underground abyss,
a light flickers throughout the length of the
tunnel, a smile sweeps across your tired face
there's a sense of relief in this escapade

You think to yourself
all this while, you kept escaping the dark
but to surrender and embrace the darkness
within
is the only light at the end of the tunnel
the source of light
to love the self
so,
lie there in the dark, my friend
you're a native now
fight your way through it
because,

Self-love isn't a destination
.

.

It's a journey
the most chaotic one, by far

Balance

As a child, I looked at the moon while travelling
moving along with me
sometimes, a skyscraper would hide it
sometimes, it would disappear for a long time
it was like playing a fun game

As a teenager, I put on my headphones while
travelling
while forgetting everything else
my emotions started feeling acknowledged
I held on to them tightly

Today, as I'm adulting,
there is nothing more essential to my travelling
kit than
music and the moon
unraveling to me that
there is some balance between
holding on and letting go

Lie

Growing up
she boasted, to none but herself, of coming from
an educated upper-middle-class family
those around, struck by hunger and poverty-
weren't as lucky
though her heart poured out for them
she went hopping about life- all mighty
on the assumption that there was a safety net
around
despite this, there was no safety
the sanctity of the space within
poisoned by hate, fear and abuse by those very
whom she called family
as if to say that
all her life, she lived a lie
thinking she had it all, had the best
only to come to a grave realisation one day
that she's the unluckiest
the poorest of them all

Pocket Tools

When the storm of thoughts runs down your
mind
with each breath burdening the chest
pause and breathe
1..2..5, 1..2..5

When your mind goes numb
and you can hardly feel
pause and notice
any four objects you can see

When all you want to do is sleep
and yet can't fall asleep
think of three places
you've always wanted to visit

When everything fails
and you want to run somewhere far
recollect the two reasons
that have kept you sane so far

When it's too difficult to keep going and easier
to end it all
just for once, hold yourself like a baby
and swing in your own arms

You are safe, loved and protected by your own
warmth

Null and Void

You are humankind's rarest possession
concerned about the bird's flight
often neglecting your own fight
using humor as a shield, you get along in life
sneaking love from your own leaky barrel
to fill up an incessant void

Breathing Thoughts

Thoughts kept flowing in
like the sea on a full moon night
and as usual, like a reservoir fine
my instinct was to block them tight

No, not this thought, I can't think that
this one's negative, you shall be damned
this one's fine, proceed with it
this one's too much, now I am pissed

Heard a voice brittle and high
sort of a newborn baby's shrill cry
let me breathe human, let me try
agreeing helplessly
I sighed

My breathing thoughts felt wild
they occupied the grounds dusty and brown
witnessing my emotional horrific tide,
they said it's okay, don't frown

As I let them breathe and took a fall
just like every other day looked at the wall
I realised they are not my foes
thoughts helped more than just cover
this darn mind felt blissful showers

Spring

So close to losing myself
when you come and hold me
as if the skies showered blooming flowers
in the dry season of fall

Race

I see you running
hell-bent on winning
something hits the ground with a sickening thud
you leave it there, don't bother to pick it up

Cheering spectators
admire your brain and brawn
their validation is all that's necessary
you win a thousand hearts

But,
Why rush?
What's this race?
.

.

If you can't even stop
to pick up
your fallen solace?

Mirrors

Brick by brick
colourful walls

Well-decorated
Well-lit

Mirrors everywhere
even on the ceiling above

Despite this
he hasn't yet seen
anyone else
even himself
somehow

He's convinced he's made a home
when all he's made
is just a house

Wholesome

Endings aren't easy
not just because it's time to leave
but because you are left with remnants and
nothing whole
broken homes, aches from broken bones

but,
broken is beautiful
cause that's when you
put in the work
and truly embark
on discovering
your wholesome soul.

www.ingramcontent.com/pod-product-compliance
Lightning Source LLC
Chambersburg PA
CBHW070735160726
48003CB00006BA/2520